a history of holding

a history of holding

poems

ALLISON MEI-LI

THIRD MOON PRESS

A History of Holding

Copyright © 2025 by Allison Mei-Li

Published by Third Moon Press
Camarillo, CA 93012

Cover and Interior Design by Allison Mei-Li
Copyedited by Kait Quinn
Author Photo by Leigha Smith

First Edition: November 2025
ISBN: 979-8-9934233-0-2 (paperback)

Printed in the United States

For Alex and Miles

TABLE OF CONTENTS

a history of holding

ELBOW DEEP

Kamakahonu, Hawaii

My son picks a clam shell from the bucket,
black and slick with brine,
bits of algae stuck to the edges,
sand packed into every crevice.

The *kamaʻāina* tells us
he picked well,
that the uglier the shell,
the prettier the pearl.

She cuts around the body with a knife,
and it opens like a mouth—
tongue of flesh,
smooth and opaque.
I sink my fingers in,
feel for the round bead buried,
whispering to my son
that I've found it.

You'll want to wash your hands, she laughs.
It'll take a while to get the stink off.

I barely hear her, though.
I'm elbow-deep
in showing my son
the heart of it all:
the muck, the rot,
the raw promise
of something beautiful.

QUICKLY, BEFORE I REMEMBER

Bring me the paper petal
of a bougainvillea,
the bit of sea glass
brought home from the beach.
Tell me about the gopher,
how he hid his head
when you made an offering
of plucked grass.
Flaunt your daffodil,
your chip of wood,
your pants that have pockets
to carry both. Let me watch you
eat a peach, dripping and sticky
down the cliff of your little chin.
I want the miracle
of a dandelion,
your breath carrying wishes
further than you can see.
Hurry, hurry—
show me the magic
before I remember
all the rest.

THE WORLD HAS NOT BEEN CRUEL
TO HIM YET

so he brings leaves to construction workers
at the park, holds them out like treasures
anyone would be glad to take. Lifts his
blue-beaded wrist up to everyone we pass,
asking, *Do you like my bracelet?*
and the only possible answer is yes.
The world has not been cruel to him yet,
so he believes there are only two types
of people—good and bad—and the bad ones
aren't real. At night, when he can't sleep,
we list out all the people who love him,
and when we run out of names, he tells me
that the trees love him. Saturn loves him.
The sky loves him too. And when he falls asleep
on my shoulder, I thank the world for staying soft
for him. For giving us a little longer.
For not being cruel to him
just yet.

LASTERDAY

My son likes to say *lasterday*,
which could mean last night,
or yesterday, or a year ago.
Tomorrow, on the other hand,
means any time that isn't right now
and hasn't happened yet.

He can't read a clock,
floats untethered to a calendar
or day of the week. Wakes up
from a nap at four p.m.
and asks, *Is it morning?*
I tell him it's not,
but he argues that the sun
is out and the joke's on me.

He measures time
in the space between two hands.
Palms pulled six inches apart,
he says, *Only be gone this long, Mama.*

The closest he gets
to a real unit of time
is holding five fingers in the air.
When I ask how long
he napped at school,
I already know the answer:
five minutes.

If I offer a half hour of playtime
at the park, he negotiates
for five minutes instead,
which to him, seems much longer—
a whole hand of fingers.

I like the way time works for him.
I want our days together to span
10,000 inches, to live in this love
for as tall as a tree. I want five minutes,
and five minutes, and five minutes more
of the pure bliss of his childhood.

I hope he will love me tomorrow
as much as he loves me today.
As much as he loved me lasterday
and the lasterday before that.

WHAT YOU'VE ALWAYS WANTED

Wake when the children wake, and not a second earlier. When their
hands find you before the sun has even climbed through the sky,
tell them you're glad they're awake. Because beneath the fog of sleep,
you are. Drag yourself to the kitchen. Brew a pot of lemon balm
and cardamom and patience. Let it steep until you unfurl like a
tea leaf. When they tug on your leg and beg you to play tiger, don't
just pretend. Become one. Roar on all fours for all the lives you left
behind, and all the selves you could have been—without them. Then
leap through the window. Sprint to the river. Lap goodness with your
greedy tongue. Watch the children wrestle in mud and grass, making
sun angels in the licks of light. Don't be surprised when their bodies
sprout into dandelions, their heads a mess of wispy fuzz. Just close
your eyes and make a wish for what you've always wanted. Remember,
what you've always wanted   is this.

PREMONITIONS IN MY POCKET

Pregnant women always made me
cry—each round belly, an omen,
a buoyant reminder
of a life I might never
hold. I carried only

premonitions in my pocket,
let them bring me
to my knees every spring.
I learned to point a finger

at my own reflection,
to trace the outline
of my body
like a crime scene.

I remember a therapist asking,
If you could stand before your body,
would you push it? Punch it?
Let out your rage?

But I had no fists left
to clench, only knots
inside my chest.

I'd get on my knees and beg, I said.
I'd fall to the floor
and ask why, why, why?

[SEARCH HISTORY, I]

what causes ovarian cysts?
how did my cyst grow to the size of a grapefruit?
fertility after ovarian surgery
reddit: trying to conceive

---

internal bleeding after cyst removal
7 transfusions = how much blood loss?
losing 40% of your body's blood
recovering from a near-death experience

---

face goes numb every night
operating room flashbacks when trying to sleep
am i hyperventilating?
how to stop a panic attack

---

what to watch when you have PTSD
movies that don't involve death
bath salts / guided meditation / essential oils / anxiety coloring books
therapists near me

---

how to know if you ovulated
why am i not ovulating?
trigger shots for fertility
where to inject hCG
[youtube: injecting hCG on your own body]

---

reddit: is this a faint line?
reddit: my faint line is getting fainter
how to save a fading pregnancy
is there anything i can do?

---

was my "chemical pregnancy" a miscarriage?
birthstone jewelry for pregnancy loss
halsey miscarriage lyrics "i've loved you for all of my life"

---

how to tell your family you lost a baby
when they never even knew
you were pregnant

WHISPER

As a child, I searched
for meaning everywhere.
In the cursive fall of a leaf,
the cloudy bruise on a pear,
lines carved into cement
like a secret language.
My little soul clung like ivy
to anything the world might offer:
the scattered line of pelicans mid-sky,
the date on a penny in the dirt.
As a child, I wanted everything
to mean something.
Truth is, I still do.
Truth is, I'm still searching—
waiting for the wind
to whisper back.

SEARCHING ON THE PCH

A crystal sun dangles
from the rearview
glinting gold,
painting sparks of light
that dance along my cheeks.

Out the window
the blur of cars
becomes a school of fish—
all of us moving together,
each of us
the same.

Tell me,
is anyone else here driving
with a hand over a womb
that won't obey,

whispering *please*
again and again,
weaving
hope and grief
into one?

WHAT THE NURSE SAID

When the nurse said, *You are pregnant,*
she threaded a question through every syllable,
left something unspoken in the air.

[*You* are *pregnant . . .*]

The day before, I'd driven to my husband's office,
pregnancy tests—pink and positive—trembling
in my hands, called him outside and recorded

his reaction: the joy-cracked cadence of his voice,
how his arms circled me like an oath. Sometimes
I still rewatch it, the moment pressed like a leaf between pages.

[*. . . but you'll be testing negative in three days.*]

There is a quiet logic to heartbreak,
how bones always brace for the fall,
grief waiting in the body like muscle memory.

So I was grateful for even a morsel, a dizzy flutter
of hope, the chance to touch my womb and not feel
empty. For three days, I was a mother,

sore breasts and nausea—not proof of life
inside me, but the cruel trick of hormones,
a body's brutal countdown.

On the third night, my husband and I went to dinner,
a distraction from the slow drip of despair,
the weight of grief pressing in on my ribs.

To the waiter, we were just another table.
Special occasion? he asked.
The seconds passed,

slow and stretched,
before I nodded and said,
Just life.

ARS POETICA
After Isabelle Correa

I don't want to write a poem

I want to birth a poem

coax it to life
under a full moon
screaming

swaddle a poem
in muslin cloth

stay up all night
watching its chest rise

let it make
me crazy

I want to feed a poem
my milk and blood

til I have nothing left
to call my own

I want to bathe a poem
bend and bruise myself
for a poem

cradle its soft spot
in my open hands

hold it to my chest
and whisper names

for all the beautiful things
around us

I want to help a poem stand
on its own two legs

then let it leave me
before I'm ready

feel my arms go empty
as I watch it walk away

carrying something
bigger

than the sound
of my voice

[SEARCH HISTORY, II]

am i more fertile after a miscarriage?
do i really have to wait three months?
what are the odds of a second pregnancy loss?
best prenatal vitamins

---

reddit: is this a faint line?
natural remedies for nausea
reducing pregnancy anxiety

---

is coffee ok?
is deli meat ok?
can i use a hot tub while pregnant?
do i need to sleep on my back?

---

covid rates near me
pregnant - what happens if i get sick?
can my husband be in the delivery room?
do i need a mask during labor?

---

how often should i feel the baby kick?
how to know if the baby is still there
what happens if a baby gets sick?

---

can my baby sense my fear?
can my baby hear my voice?
can my baby feel my heartbeat?

ORIGIN STORY

My son used to be a star
I wished upon.
When the sky dripped
ink and indigo,
I crept, half-lidded,
to the living room.
Played the music

that made me
a river. Swayed
my empty body,
praying to the moon
like she was a woman

who could understand.
I could've sworn
I saw her face,
but then
I could've sworn
a lot of things—

that I swallowed a star
every night
and grew it alive
in my sleep,
but always,
it was just a dream,
until one day

I woke to warmth,
hope splitting me full
at the seams.

EARTHSIDE

The darkness of night hung in balance
with the glow of fluorescence,
electricity buzzing through my heavy legs.
I craned forward, shoulders curved
toward bursting belly, bent in prayer
for the universe
    of my own body,
for the planet
    in the center of my abdomen.
When the earth quaked,
his slippery body emerged,
slick and curled,
a heaving chest of cries.
They placed him in my arms
and clamped our tether,
making him whole,
breaking me open in two.
I could say my womb became emptier
without him,
but he left behind the light
of one million shimmering moons.

THE FIRST NIGHT

I didn't sleep, didn't even try,
groggy with awe and adrenaline.

For hours, I watched him,
bundled and beanied,
new as daybreak,
soft as dusk.

My body collapsed,
wilted as a plucked wildflower,
burnt out like the last match.
Exhaustion thrummed
through every nerve,
and still I couldn't
close my eyes.

Can you imagine
turning away
from your first sunrise?

I'd never seen
anything
shine so bright.

AFTERSHOCK

Once, we were two: a tiny universe
spinning on red wine and chapped lips,

our love like a screeching halt,
a red light that you nearly miss.

We used to lay on the floor,
cheek to cheek, legs pointing

to different poles of the globe;
we were the whole world—

until the sky said try,
the stars said beg,

and we thought of nothing else
but the soft spot of a newborn in June.

I remember the night the dream came true:
you in the corner, our baby wrapped in your arms

and me—trapped in the hospital bed,
stars skittering behind my eyelids.

It wasn't what I pictured.

I reached for you in the aftershock,
the way I always had before

but our universe of two
had stretched past its prime,

widened the waiting mouth
of love, and now

there were three
there were three
there were
         three.

BORN

I limped around the house,
bruised and milk-stained,
while my mother whisked
around the kitchen, steeping
teas of ginger and cinnamon,
hibiscus, dark as blood—
her tonic to heal my body.

When I wasn't marveling
at the rise and fall of the baby's chest,
I was worrying myself into a winter.
Every sunset brought a bouquet
of dread. Every dinner plate
was a thing to cry into.
I was always hungry for air,
rushing outside, palms open,
trying to catch my breath.

The baby blues, they all said,
but nothing felt pastel.
I'd fallen into the deep end,
bottomless and murky as ash,
like the time I got lost
in the current at Black Rock.
And again, it was my mother
who pulled me ashore.

She was the only one
who could reach me.
She knew what the rest didn't—
that my baby
was not the only one
who had just been born.

[SEARCH HISTORY, III]

why do i cry when the sun sets?
baby blues vs. postpartum depression
roller coaster sensation at night
why isn't motherhood what i thought it would be?

---

baby never sleeps
are there diapers that don't leak?
why are my lips and eyes swelling?
do antihistamines dry out breast milk?

---

heart pounds when i lay down
my sound machine sounds like a choir
hearing things: am i going crazy?

---

is it ok if i don't breastfeed?
reddit: formula-fed babies
healthiest organic baby formula

---

instant ice maxi pads
postpartum depression quiz
do mom support groups exist?
how long can you go without sleep?
body feels like it's shutting down

---

how to feel safe in my body
how to treat postpartum depression
how to know if i'm a good mom

WORD BANK FOR THE BABY BLUE(S)

Baby blue like forget-me-nots, the dainty blooms
of an azure aster, denim cut-offs and snow cones,
the bedspread in your teenage room. Baby blue
like low tide, clear as bathwater, or the sky
on a cloudless day. Cotton candy, vintage tea cups,
the shade of a day dream at noon. Baby blue(s)
like the calm as it spins into chaos, the tint of a secret
you can't admit, tears mixing with the shower water,
a siren glowing through an empty town. Baby blues
like the monitor screaming, lips tinged from being left out
in the cold, the fog of your vision blurring, the shadow
of your face as you drown.

NO ONE'S MOTHER

Every morning   I am someone's mother.   Someone's dish rag

disheveled   on the floor.   I am   keeping my head

above water—   kind of.   I don't know if my cup

is empty   or half-full.   I am pouring.   I am wrung.

I am honestly done.   But sometimes,   on a Tuesday,

when the light hums   through our bedroom shutters,

my body   below yours   becomes something   to hold

and your hands   grip my skin   like I am   finally whole

and for a moment,   I   am

        no one's   mother   at all.

FOUR DAYS IN

Quantum entanglement occurs when two particles become linked on a subatomic level, affecting one another regardless of distance or time.

I stripped down to my skin,
alone and bare as the day I began,
the shower door closing
like a cathedral,
my body puddling into peace
for the first time in days.

I heard nothing but water
trickling to the floor,
saw nothing but steam
rising with abandon,

and still

I could *feel* my baby cry,
with his curled legs
and milky breath,
little back arching
in protest.

I felt him
the way a stomach drops
before an earthquake,
or a joint stiffens
as the rain rolls in.

Maybe it's just
physics—

I've been split
in two: he and I,
now echoes
of one another,

speaking in secret
as if tethered
by a whisper.

And even when
I evaporate someday,
become a speck
of dust in the sky,

I'll stay bound
forever
to the tender ache
of this love.

LOVE POEM

He says he doesn't love me,
but he does *like* me.
You're just not the best, he says—gently,
like it hurts him to break my heart.
There's no time to catch my breath
before he yells at me
for my dance moves,
for singing with the radio,
for making him laugh.
He didn't want to laugh.
Maybe that's why he thinks
he doesn't love. At dinner,
he throws food on the ground,
cheeks turning tomato.
I am too tired to clean
so I leave it, let the leftover bits
turn to husk overnight.
Back aching, I wrestle him
into pajamas before bed,
the weight of the day
pressing on my temples.
Hey, what do you think 'love' is? I ask.
His face becomes a window.
He smiles at me and says,
You.

MOTHER TONGUE

Whoever said there are only five love languages
never met my grandmother. She loved

in the language of worry—sleepless nights
and newspaper clippings sealed neatly into

cream envelopes: headlines like *Bagged Lettuce Can Kill*
and *Family Dead by Unattended Stove.*

When I went hunting for my first house,
she tossed and turned til 2 a.m., afraid

I'd find a home too large to clean. I felt
guilty keeping her up like that, knew

she was helpless to the heat of concern.
How do I explain this to someone

who doesn't worry over sleepovers
or school security, sickness or strangers

on lonely playgrounds? You ask why
motherhood made a spider of me—

spinning scenarios into sticky webs,
latching onto any fears that flutter in.

But listen, I am not the spider.
I'm the one trapped inside the web.

LISTEN TO ME

There is not a single sliver of my body
that does not know your name,
that has not memorized
the tangle of your limbs
or the way your hair falls
across your face

and oh my god,
it hurts

   how anything
   can happen.

Every morning,
more photographs
from overseas—
mothers holding babies
like bones, starved
of mercy and hope.

Another drill
for active shooters
at your school—
all of you hiding
and huddled
beneath your tiny
wooden desks.

Aren't we all just balancing
on a pinhead,
a stroke of luck
until it turns the other way?

Oh god,
I just remembered

none of us
have control.

How cruel,
that I can bring you
into this world

and not know
if I can keep you
here.

NOCTURNAL

A mother's body is primed

    to be alert,

        to wake in the dark, panting,

            vigilant.

                Dread

        takes root in her belly,

      slithers around her

    insides like ivy,

fills the corners

    of her mind with fear.

      Something unseen stirs,

    feeding on the silence,

      alive in the middle of the

           night.

THE WOMEN

In another life, we don't meet
by the chicken coop at the farm

or the children's shelves of the library.
We don't find each other

through the white hum of a bounce house
or the crowd at the edge of the harbor.

There are no therapy sessions
disguised as playdates

or tired nights spent side by side,
spilling secrets like wine.

I never learn how to unmask, to dive
down the ski slope of truth, to admit

Sometimes I hide in the bathroom
and hear you say, *Me too.*

There are no doorstep deliveries
of orange juice or cough syrup,

no porch light intentionally left on.
In another life, I never know friendship

like ours. So thank goodness
we're in this life—and not that one.

SWALLOW

The other women tell me I'm not alone in my rage,
share suggestions like they're swapping family
recipes—First, throw eggs. Then, bash
windows. Next, smash porcelain
plates. Let something else
be broken.
But I
don't
break a thing,
and neither do they,
unless you count breaking
our own hearts. We'd choose flight,
but we've never outrun anything. We'd
choose fight, but we have nothing left to give.
So we swallow anger whole. Let it burn the backs
of our throats. Dab the corners of our mouths with a rag.

TELLTALE SIGNS

"Oh, you don't look like a mom!"
— Woman at the doctor's office

She says I don't look like a mom,
and for a heartbeat,
I almost say *thank you,*
gratitude rising like a reflex
for a gift I'm supposed to want.

Because isn't that the dream—
to look untouched
by the firm grip of motherhood,
as if my body
never rearranged itself
to make room
for a foot or a throat?

But all the signs are here.
She's just missed them,
so I bring her closer,
tell her to look again

at the soft give of my stomach,
stretched and loosened by love,
the worry line etched
by my left eyebrow,
how it's folded my face
into a poem.

Look again
at the shape of my arms.
Isn't it obvious
what they've held?
Can't you tell?
They've cradled
a whole world.

SEAWEED QUEEN

You place a tangle of kelp
atop my head,

anoint me seaweed queen,
serve me crab-

shaped cookies
made of sand.

The world inside
my screen beckons,

but I spend
the whole afternoon

tracing sunlight
as it twirls

on the tiny blades
of your shoulders.

THE FINE PRINT

We hereby declare you the Mother of yet-unknown Child. This contract automatically renews on the Child's birth date each year.

Exclusions and Restrictions Apply: Not valid in conjunction with long showers, international travel, white rugs, or breakable ceramic.

Eligibility: Must be able to operate on very little sleep, use the bathroom with the door open, multitask through noise exceeding 120 decibels, and produce a bottomless well of empathy.

Time Limits: You may receive reminders from persons at the coffee shop that "It All Goes So Fast"; however, the absence of such reminders does not permit the Mother to forget.

Amendments: Your role and responsibilities are subject to change without notice. Please note that the Child may undergo significant personality shifts at yearly, monthly, daily, or hourly intervals.

Return Policy: The Child comes as is. Please do your best to meet the specific needs of your Child, which will differ from those of other Children.

Side Effects: May include swirls of hair in the drain, the snap of nerves and tendons, heart stretch and altered vision, intrusive thoughts at 3 a.m., and joy as a sixth sense. You may find the world more haunting, dangerous, broken, magical, beautiful, and deeper than you have previously known.

MOM GUILT

In a dream, I ride shotgun
in the silver bullet of a sedan,
knuckles the color of bone,
wheels clipping the side of a cliff.
I scream just before we tumble
from the knife's edge of the road,
sixty feet down, flying
through the front door
of someone's house.

Dream interpretation says
I should lose some teeth now,
so my molars—all four—
rainfall out of my mouth,
just as I tell the police
none of this is my fault.

How could it be?
        I wasn't even driving.

Still, I lean my body
against the trunk,
rehearse apologies,
drawn like a moth
to the blame.
I am a magnet
for every pointed finger.
Just tell me what I could have
done better

and I will accept,
like any good mother,
that all signs point
to me.

IF A MOM SAID, "I JUST CAN'T TODAY"
AND THE DAY ACTUALLY LISTENED

The day would whistle, call it off,
curl its corners inward, snapping
at the center like a bedsheet,
apologetic and rolled up tidy.
She'd carry it to the washing machine,
set it to the opposite of "gentle"
because this day deserves to be tumbled
hot and high. To be scrubbed clean
of all the crumbs and unsolicited advice,
guilt stifling as a greenhouse in July.
Once the day was washed and warmed,
she'd sling it across the kitchen chairs,
shut it down like a TV screen,
easy as the click of a button.
Watch it turn black and opaque,
with just enough glare
to see her reflection.
Finally, enough silence
to hear her own thoughts,
to know, underneath it all,
she's still here.

THOUGH I HAVE FORGOTTEN

A group of men lift their eyes
when I walk into the coffee shop.

It's summer and I am wearing
a dress. Summer, and I am alone,

no child wrapped around my calves,
legs bare for the first time

in months. Suddenly, I'm aware
of my surroundings—

aware, again, that I am
still a woman,

though I have forgotten
so many times.

I order a matcha,
toss in something sweet

because these twenty minutes alone
are supposed to save me.

At a table in the corner,
I flip through Ellen Bass,

pretend the clock isn't breathing
down my neck.

I try not to watch the children
running past the window,

a reminder of what waits
for me at home.

A man from the group looks up again
to smile at me, and I'm not sure

what he thinks he sees,
but I guess I could be anyone.

Summer, and I could still be
anyone.

EVERY DAY OPENS

Ever since he found our cat
curled into stillness

and watched the hawk swoop in
on the unsuspecting squirrel,

ever since we stood open-mouthed
beneath a tower of dinosaur bones,

my son has been curious
about death.

He asks me often
whether something can die—

Can plants? Can toys? Can stars?
Turns out, almost anything can.

One day, we sit cross-legged
on the kitchen floor, our knees

kissed by pools of light,
and he starts the game again:

Can fruit die?
Can cars die?

And then,
Will we die?

Lately, every day opens into a choice,
where I may keep him

small or let him know
the way this world works.

I tell him the truth.
Then he asks, in a hush,

*How much time
do we have left?*

I tell him,
We have so much time

even though
it will never be

enough.

THE HEART CEREMONY

When someone you love dies,
you imagine the world reacting—

maybe the sky rains down in condolence.
Maybe the ocean pulls back like a blanket,

or everyone else vanishes and only you are left
to do whatever grief demands.

But the day my grandmother dies,
we find ourselves at Build-A-Bear.

Because the calendar says so.
Because there is nothing else to do

but let my toddler run in circles,
oblivious to our sudden loss.

Turns out there is no pause button
on parenting, so I arrange myself

into something my son will recognize,
and stand in line amid a sea of hollow bears.

We wait and wait and wait,
though I don't believe in time anymore;

don't understand how she could
be here yesterday and not today.

When it's our turn, a woman
hands me a heart sewn of satin.

I turn it over in my palm,
tiny and precious as a prayer,

press it like a talisman
to my chest.

Now make a wish and seal it with a kiss
before we place this heart inside your bear.

At last, a place to put it—

all the ache,
the weight,
the leftover love

stitched into something
that can hold it.

A MOON, A SUN, A PILE OF LAUNDRY

Let me explain—
you are plunged
into this world
water-logged
and language-less,
no control over where
you come up.

If you are lucky,
most days will be ordinary,
deliciously predictable:
a moon, a sun,
a pile of laundry,
someone who follows you
through the front door.

If you are lucky,
you might grow old,
wrinkled with every reason,
a collector of good days,
the well-worn kind
that soften
the most broken,
brittle bits.

AT THE COFFEE SHOP, A STRANGER TELLS ME ABOUT THE "GREATEST GIFT"

"The greatest gift you can give your child is a sibling."
— Woman with the chai latte

But what about sunrises
swept over dotted hills,

or a kitchen table
by the bay window
set for three,

fingers dipped
into low tide's
opal waters,

our backs pressed
to firm ground
beneath the stars?

What about the arms
that hold him
through every kind of winter

or the strawberries
we pluck straight
off the vine?

This world we've built
together is more than
I could have dreamed.

Believe me,
the greatest gift
is each other.

THE SCENIC ROUTE

Go on, take the broom—
even if you miss the dustpan,
crumbs scattering like birdseed
on a windy day.
I love to watch you try.
I have always been one
for the scenic route.

Let us hold hands
down the grocery aisle,
tapping our chins as we take in
the art installation
of cereal boxes.
Forget the self-checkout
at the library,
let us carry each book
in the crooks of our arms
to the woman with the tattooed wrist,
the one who hands you stickers
like magic from a sleeve.

Let us spill the pancake batter,
watch it spread, spelling m-e-s-s:
a word that no longer alarms me.
Little one, let's do this together.
Even if it takes three times
as long. I have nowhere
better to be
than here,
dancing with you
in the soft belly
of this slow life.

THE FIRST DENT

A boy says *no* when my son asks
to play, and everything inside me
breaks. Not the swift shatter of glass
against tile, but a mountain's slow crumble:
whiplashed by wind, worn down by waves.

The facade slips from the cliff of me,
and again, I am a girl alone,
shoving twigs into gopher holes
of hope. A teen flattened against the wall,
waiting to be asked to dance.
I am a woman under the moon,
begging for life to sprout,
and all I can do now
is watch my child blink,
a pause that fills with questions
he doesn't yet know how to ask.

I wonder if he feels it,
this first crack
hissing like ice on a pond—
the truth pressing
through the surface,
making its very first dent.

IF I HAD MY OWN

He keeps a nature shelf in his room
of rocks and shells and pine cones,
dried dandelions and twigs.
A time capsule of his treasures.

If I had my own,
I'd keep the freckle under his right eye,
the drops of ice cream from his chin,
his insistence on wearing jeans and socks,
even at the beach.

I'd keep his voice from the backseat
cheering *skinny moon!*
when a crescent hangs in the sky
and *the bright went away!*
when the sun dips behind a cloud.

I'd keep the blanket we lay
on our bodies each morning,
the hooded towel
with the puppy ears after bath.
I'd keep his hand in mine,
his arm around my neck,
his weight in the curve of my lap.

TEXTS I ALMOST SEND MY SON BEFORE
I REMEMBER HE DOESN'T HAVE A PHONE

Hey. Sorry I was so cranky this morning. It's the 5 a.m.
wake ups you know? Maybe we could talk about moving
that to a different time?

Omg I just saw a trash truck lol

What did they give you for snack?

Hey can you please try to nap today?

Sorry I didn't read that extra story last night.

I'm thinking of you.

I love you.

I'll be there soon.

EVERYTHING, EVEN A SHADOW

My son laces his fingers
through mine and says,

Your hands are smaller than Daddy's,
so your hands must still be growing.

I turn my palms up—
all lifelines and crossroads,
a history of everything
I've held.

No, love, I say,
my hands are all done.
This is how they will always be.

He peers up at me sideways,
doubtful, as if he knows
that nothing ever stays
the same.

After all, he is growing out of
his favorite clothes and into
the next classroom,
hair falling over his eyes
every six weeks,

and the roses in our yard keep
pressing toward the sky,
the lima beans still sprouting
on the window sill.

Everything, even a shadow,
stretches as the sun falls,
spilling silently
across the ground.

So maybe I shouldn't tell him
that my hands will never change

when every day,
they learn the shape
of letting go.

ACKNOWLEDGMENTS

I'd like to express my deepest gratitude to the following people:

To my writing communities—thank you for the inspiration, support, and magic. It has been a gift to write alongside you.

Heidi Fiedler, thank you for showing me how to bring ease and gentleness to the publishing process, and for being a true teammate in this otherwise solitary venture. I am so grateful for your wisdom and friendship.

Jillian Stacia, you treated this collection like it was your own. Thank you for your incredible insight, for keeping me tethered throughout this process, and for making me laugh along the way. This experience would not have been the same without you.

I am thankful to my early readers—Ashlee Gadd, Elise Powers, Michelle Awad, Ophelia Monet, Heidi Fiedler, Jillian Stacia, and Leslie Wong—for taking the time to read and reflect on this collection with me. Thank you, Kait Quinn, for your attentive editing, and Kelly Grace Thomas, for pushing me to go deeper.

I could not write a book on motherhood without thanking the village that supported me. Hannah, Rose, Heryka, and Daya—thank you for caring for my son with such kindness; you are angels on earth. To *Mama Bloom* and *Exhale*, thank you for the guidance, support, and compassion you've shown to mothers like me.

Valerie Soto, Ashley LaFevers, Kristen Weld, and Jessica Batres—thank you for reminding me how much this book matters. I can't imagine doing motherhood without you.

To my parents, who transcribed my thoughts into a diary before I could write them down myself—you showed me that my words and my voice mattered. Thank you to my mom, Leslie, for giving me a tender heart, and to my dad, Brian, for inspiring me to chase my dreams. To my late Grandma Stella, thank you for championing my writing with all the enthusiasm in the world. I know you are somewhere clapping the loudest.

Most of all, thank you to my soulmate, Alex. With you, anything feels possible. Thank you for carrying this dream alongside me and making sure I had the time, space, and encouragement to bring this book into the world. I'm endlessly grateful for you and for the life we're building together.

And to my son, Miles—my soulchild—thank you for making me a mom. I love you more than you will ever know. You are the one I wanted.

NOTES

I am grateful to the editors of the following journals where these poems first appeared, sometimes in earlier versions or with alternate titles.

"Quickly, Before I Remember" – *The Wild Umbrella*

"The World Has Not Been Cruel to Him Yet" – *Rust & Moth*

"Lasterday" – *wildscape*

"Searching on the PCH" – *Coffee + Crumbs* (as "Crystal Sun")

"Ars Poetica" – *MER Literary* (as "I Don't Want to Write a Poem"), a response to Isabelle Correa's "I Don't Want to Write a Poem"

"Earthside" – *Coffee + Crumbs* (as "One Million Shimmering Moons")

"Born" – *Voicemail Poems*

"The Scenic Route" – *Coffee + Crumbs*

"The First Dent" – *The Wild Umbrella*

"If I Had My Own" – *wildscape*

"Everything, Even a Shadow" – *wildscape*

ABOUT THE AUTHOR

Allison Mei-Li is a writer, mother, and speech-language pathologist based in Southern California. Her work has appeared in anthologies, podcasts, and journals such as *Rust & Moth, Coffee + Crumbs, MER Literary, Voicemail Poems, wildscape,* and more.

Web: writtenbyallison.com
Instagram: @writtenbyallison
Substack: writtenbyallison.substack.com

www.ingramcontent.com/pod-product-compliance
Lightning Source LLC
Chambersburg PA
CBHW020806130626
46554CB00006B/2312